The Story of
ISAAC and JACOB

By REV. JUDE WINKLER, OFM Conv.

P9-EGC-304

Imprimi Potest: **Daniel Pietrzak, OFM Conv.**, Minister Provincial of St. Anthony of Padua Province (USA)
Nihil Obstat: **Daniel V. Flynn, J.C.D.**, Censor Librorum
Imprimatur: **Patrick J. Sheridan**, Vicar General, Archdiocese of New York

The birth of Isaac

ABRAHAM and Sarah, the mother and father of the people of Israel, were very special friends of God. He showed His love for them by making a covenant with them. God promised that He would bless them and their descendants forever.

Yet Abraham and Sarah did not have any children, and they had grown very old. So Sarah sent her servant, Hagar, in to be with Abraham so that she might have a child whom she could adopt. Hagar gave birth to a son whom she named Ishmael.

But God was going to fulfill His promise in a truly wonderful way. He and two angels visited the camp of Abraham and Sarah. Abraham, who thought that they were three men traveling along, invited them to stop and eat with him. God blessed Abraham for his goodness, and He promised Abraham and Sarah that they would have a son by that time the next year.

Abraham and Sarah had a very difficult time believing that God would perform this miracle. They even laughed at the idea that they would have a child when Abraham was one hundred years old and Sarah ninety years old. God was true to His promise. The next year Sarah and Abraham had a son whom they named Isaac. They blessed the Lord for this special gift.

One day Sarah saw Ishmael, the son of Hagar, the slave woman, playing with her son Isaac. Sarah became frightened for she thought that Ishmael might try to harm Isaac in order to inherit the promise given to Abraham. She asked Abraham to send Ishmael and his mother away so that Isaac might be safe and be the only one to inherit the promise.

Abraham did not want to do this, but God ordered Abraham to listen to her. So Abraham prepared a bit of food and water for Hagar and Ishmael and sent them off into the desert.

God tests Abraham

NOW that Abraham had sent Ishmael away, he had only one son who could inherit the promise that God had given to him: Isaac.

One day God put Abraham to the test. He said to Abraham, "Take your son, Isaac, your only one, whom you love, and go to the land of Moriah. There you shall offer him up as a holocaust on a mountain that I will point out to you."

Abraham was very confused and troubled by this request. God had promised him a son and He had already ordered him to send one son away. Now he was ordering Abraham to sacrifice his only remaining son, a boy whom he dearly loved.

Yet, Abraham obeyed God. He took his son and two servants and set off for the place where he was to sacrifice Isaac. It took them three days to reach that place. When they arrived, Abraham ordered the servants to remain with the donkeys, and he and Isaac climbed the mountain alone.

On the way, Abraham carried the fire and knife for he feared that Isaac might harm himself (a sign of how much he loved the boy).

When they reached the top of the mountain, Abraham tied up his son and put him on the altar that he had built. He was ready to sacrifice him when an angel appeared and ordered him not to harm the boy. The angel told Abraham that God now knew how much he loved Him.

God was so pleased with all that Abraham had done that He made him a promise. God told Abraham that he would have so many descendants that there would be more of them than there were stars in the sky or sand on the shore of the sea.

A wife is found for Isaac

WHEN Sarah died, Abraham realized that it was time for him to find a wife for his son Isaac. He did not want Isaac to marry any of the pagan women of Canaan, so he sent a servant back to his homeland to find a wife for him.

The servant prayed to God and asked Him to point out which woman was to be Isaac's wife. He asked for a sign: that the woman who was to marry Isaac would not only give water to him and his men but also offer to give water to his camels.

He then went to the well in the city of Nahor. That evening the women of the city came out to fill their jars with water from the well. One of them, Rebekah, was a beautiful and generous young woman.

When the servant asked Rebekah for a drink, she offered to give him water and to water his camels as well, just as the servant had prayed to God.

Abraham's servant went to Rebekah's house and talked to her family. He explained to them how Abraham had sent him to this city to find a wife for his son and how he had prayed for a sign. He told them that Rebekah had done all that he had asked for as a sign from the Lord.

Rebekah marries Isaac

ABRAHAM'S servant gave Rebekah's family all of the gifts that he had brought along. He then asked them whether Rebekah might travel back to Canaan with him to be the wife of his master's son.

Rebekah's family was very pleased with all that had been said. They asked Rebekah if she would be willing to go with the servant to marry Isaac.

Rebekah knew that the trip was very long and that she might never see her family again, but she was a very generous woman. She agreed to leave her homeland to become Isaac's wife.

So Abraham's servant brought Rebekah back with him to Canaan. Isaac was in the field one night when he saw the camels of Abraham's servant approaching. Rebekah, too, saw Isaac from a distance and she put on her veil, as women of that time were supposed to do when they were meeting their future husbands.

The servant told Isaac everything that had happened to him in Nahor and how God pointed Rebekah out to him. Isaac was filled with joy when he heard all this and he married Rebekah. His love for Rebekah grew to be a very deep love, and she became the center of his life.

Isaac's firstborn son is a hunter

FOR a long time Rebekah did not have any children, so Isaac and Rebekah prayed to the Lord. He heard their prayers, and Rebekah became pregnant with twins. While the twins were still in her womb, they fought with each other, a sign of what would happen between them.

When the children were born, the older brother had red hair and he was named Esau. His younger brother was born holding on to Esau's heel and he was named Jacob.

Esau was a very strong man. He liked the outdoors and so he became a hunter.

Isaac's son Jacob becomes a shepherd

JACOB, Esau's brother, did not like to hunt as his brother did. He did not like to live out in the wilds for weeks at a time and to be away from his family. For that reason, he took care of the flocks of sheep for his family and he lived in his family's tents.

Isaac loved Esau more than he loved Jacob because he used to like to eat the meals that Esau would prepare for him from the wild animals that he took. Rebekah, on the other hand, loved Jacob more than she loved Esau for he spent much more time with her in the camp than Esau did.

Esau sells his birthright

ONCE, when Jacob was preparing a meal for himself, Esau returned home from one of his hunting trips. He had been gone quite a while and was now very hungry. He saw the lentil stew that Jacob was cooking, and he wanted some of it right away.

Esau went up to Jacob and told him to give him some of the red stuff he was cooking (for lentils are red in color). He said that he needed to eat right away because he was starving to death.

Jacob was very quick in thinking. He told Esau that he would give him some of the stew if Esau would give him his rights as the firstborn. In those days the oldest son would inherit all of his father's property. Esau answered that he would give him this birthright for it would not do him any good anyway if he were to die of hunger.

So Jacob gave his brother some bread and some of the lentil stew. Esau ate it all in a hurry and then went away.

Esau was very foolish to have sold his birthright to Jacob, and Jacob was not really fair to his brother for having taken advantage of him.

Isaac digs a well

ABRAHAM had dug many wells to give water to his people and their sheep and camels. When he had died, his enemies, the Philistines, filled in many of the wells with dirt so that no one could drink from them. Now Isaac had become so rich with many people following him that he needed new wells. His servants dug out Abraham's wells and even dug new wells.

The people of that place fought with Isaac over those wells, but Isaac made a covenant with their king so that they could all live in peace.

Esau hunts for his father's meal

WHEN Isaac was very old, he called his older son to himself. He told him that he wanted to give him his special blessing before he died. First, though, he wanted Esau to go hunting and to prepare a meal from what he caught for he liked that type of food. After that he would give Esau his blessing.

While Esau was gone, Rebekah learned of what Isaac had said to Esau. She loved Jacob more than she loved Esau, and she decided that Jacob should get Isaac's blessing rather than Esau.

Jacob steals Esau's blessing

REBEKAH told Jacob everything that she had heard. She then told him how he could get his father's blessing.

Isaac was very old and was almost completely blind. She would prepare a meal just as Isaac liked from one of the kids of Jacob's flock. She would also help to disguise Jacob so that Isaac would think that he was Esau.

Rebekah prepared that meal and took Esau's best clothes and gave them to Jacob to put on. She also took the skins from the sheep that she had cooked and she put them on Jacob's hands and arms (for Esau was very hairy).

Jacob then brought the meal to Isaac, his father. Isaac was very confused for he knew that the voice he heard was Jacob's, but when he felt his hands and arms, they were hairy like Esau's.

When Isaac finished his meal, he asked his son to come closer. He smelled his clothes and he was finally convinced that it was Esau.

And so Isaac gave Jacob the special blessing that one gives a firstborn son.

Soon after this, Esau returned from hunting, and he prepared a meal for his father. But when he brought the meal to Isaac, Isaac told him that he had already given his special blessing to Esau's brother.

Esau hated his brother Jacob for all of this. Rebekah was afraid that Esau would kill his brother because of the trick that he had played on him. She told Jacob to go to her homeland to stay with her brother, Laban, until it would be safe to return.

Jacob has a powerful dream

ON the way to the city of Haran where Laban lived, Jacob stopped for the night at a special shrine.

During the night he had a dream. He saw a large staircase going up to heaven.

On the staircase Jacob saw angels going up to and down from heaven. He heard the Lord say to him that he would receive a special blessing, the blessing that had been promised to Abraham, his grandfather.

The altar at Bethel

WHEN Jacob woke up from his dream, he realized that this was a very holy place. He took the stone that he had used as a pillow and he poured oil upon it. He then set the stone up to mark this place as holy for all times. He changed the name of the place from Luz to Bethel, a name that means the house of God.

Jacob promised the Lord that if he returned from his journey in safety, the Lord would be his God forever. He would give a portion of all that he owned to the Lord all his life.

Jacob meets Rachel at the well

JACOB continued on his journey until he came to the city of Haran, the place where his mother's relatives lived.

Arriving there, he saw the well at which the shepherds there watered their sheep. On top of the well there was a large stone that could only be moved by a group of very strong men.

Jacob asked the shepherds why they did not water their sheep and then allow them to go out to the fields until it was dark. The shepherds answered that they could not uncover the well until all of their men were there, for the stone on top of it was just too big.

Just at that time Rachel, the daughter of his uncle Laban, arrived. When Jacob saw her, he went over and rolled the stone off the top of the well by himself. He then watered all the sheep that belonged to his uncle.

When he had finished watering the sheep, Jacob went over to Rachel and kissed her. He burst into tears for he was filled with joy to find out that she was his relative. He told Rachel all about himself, and she led him to her house where Laban, her father, greeted Jacob and invited him to stay with them.

Caring for Laban's flock

JACOB cared for the sheep that belonged to Laban for a full month. When Laban asked him what pay he wanted, Jacob answered that he would like to marry Laban's younger daughter, Rachel, for he had fallen in love with her.

Laban said that Jacob should work for him for seven years and when that period of time had been completed, he would give Jacob Rachel's hand in marriage. When Jacob had finished his seven years of service, he went to Laban and asked him to fulfill the promise he had made to allow Rachel to marry him.

Jacob marries Leah

LABAN prepared a wedding feast for Jacob. But instead of giving him Rachel, Laban gave Jacob her older sister, Leah. Jacob did not know he was marrying the wrong woman for she was wearing a veil. When he found out, he complained to Laban that he had been cheated.

Laban answered Jacob that he had done what was necessary, for in their country the older sister always married before the younger sister. If he wanted to marry Rachel, he could work for him another seven years as her price.

Jacob marries Rachel

JACOB was so in love with Rachel that he agreed to work for Laban for another seven years.

After that second period of seven years, he finally married Rachel, the woman whom he loved.

Jacob now had two wives (for in those days a man could marry more than one woman). He loved Rachel greatly, but he did not really love her sister, Leah. This made Leah very sad.

The Lord saw how sad Leah was and He blessed her, allowing her to have a son whom she named Reuben. She had other sons, too, and she named them Simeon, Levi, and Judah. Meanwhile, Rachel had no children.

When Rachel saw that she could have no children of her own, she decided to let her servant go into Jacob's tent so that she would have a child whom Rachel could adopt. Her servant had a son whom she named Dan and another son whom she named Naphtali.

Leah then sent her own servant into Jacob's tent. Her servant bore two sons whom she named Gad and Asher. All the while Rachel was still barren. She even bought a plant from Reuben, Leah's son, in the hope that the plant would help her to bear children—but it did not.

Instead, Leah became pregnant once again and had another son whom she named Issachar. She called a sixth son Zebulun and then had a daughter whom she named Dinah.

God finally listened to the prayers of Rachel, and she bore a son. She named her son Joseph. Jacob now had eleven sons and one daughter, but his favorite child of all was Joseph for he loved his mother, Rachel, in a very special way.

Jacob obtains a flock of his own

AFTER Jacob had worked for seven years for Leah and seven years for Rachel, he began to work for a portion of the flock. One year he would work for all of the spotted lambs that would be born in the flock and another year he would work for those that were not spotted.

God blessed Jacob and his part of the flock increased greatly. Jacob's flock became so large that Laban's family became jealous of him. They were ready to accuse him of stealing their flock from them. Jacob decided to return to his home-land before there would be trouble.

Jacob wrestles with God

ON his way back to Canaan, Jacob planned what he would say to his brother Esau. He knew that Esau was very angry with him, and he was afraid.

The night before he met Esau, Jacob had a dream in which he was wrestling with an angel. He could not beat the angel, and the angel could not beat him. They wrestled all night, and in the morning he asked for the angel's blessing before letting him go. The angel was really God, Who blessed him and gave him a new name, Israel.

In the morning Jacob limped away for he had been hurt while he was wrestling.

Jacob makes peace with Esau

JACOB was always tricking people, and it seems as if he was planning to try to trick Esau when he met him. But once Jacob met God face to face, he knew he could not lie to Esau anymore. He would have to be honest with him.

The next morning, Jacob went out and bowed before his brother Esau. Esau ran to meet Jacob, embraced him, and wept. He forgave him for tricking him so many years before and stealing their father's blessing from him.

Jacob and Esau each went his own way along with all of their people and belongings. Jacob thanked God for bringing him home safely.

Rachel and Isaac die

JACOB and Rachel had one more child after this, giving Jacob twelve sons. Rachel died while giving birth. Before she died, she said she wanted her son named Ben-oni, which meant "son of her sorrow," for she knew she was dying.

Instead, Jacob named him Benjamin, the son of the south. Jacob buried his beloved wife near Bethlehem. Jacob later camped near Hebron and while he was there his father, Isaac, died. Jacob and Esau buried their father next to Sarah.

Jacob and his twelve sons

JACOB lived for many years after this. Of his twelve sons, he loved his youngest two sons, (Benjamin and Joseph) the best for they were Rachel's children. He even gave Joseph a special coat as a sign of his love.

Jacob's other sons were jealous because of the special love that Jacob showed his youngest sons. One day when Joseph came to visit them in the fields, they threw him in a well and later sold him into slavery in Egypt.

Joseph lived as a slave in Egypt for many years. Then the Lord saved him from his misery. Pharaoh had a dream that Joseph was able to interpret. Pharaoh was so impressed that he made Joseph an important leader in Egypt. Joseph was placed in charge of all the food in the entire land.

Later, when there was a terrible famine over all the earth, Joseph was able to save his family. He forgave his brothers and brought them and his father to Egypt. By forgiving his brothers, he taught them how to love, and in turn they were able to forgive their father for not having loved them as much as he should have.

Jacob died there many years later surrounded by his children and grandchildren.

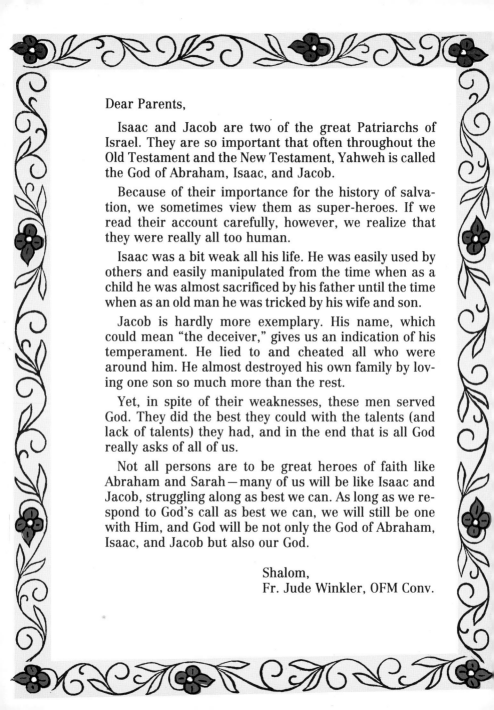

Dear Parents,

Isaac and Jacob are two of the great Patriarchs of Israel. They are so important that often throughout the Old Testament and the New Testament, Yahweh is called the God of Abraham, Isaac, and Jacob.

Because of their importance for the history of salvation, we sometimes view them as super-heroes. If we read their account carefully, however, we realize that they were really all too human.

Isaac was a bit weak all his life. He was easily used by others and easily manipulated from the time when as a child he was almost sacrificed by his father until the time when as an old man he was tricked by his wife and son.

Jacob is hardly more exemplary. His name, which could mean "the deceiver," gives us an indication of his temperament. He lied to and cheated all who were around him. He almost destroyed his own family by loving one son so much more than the rest.

Yet, in spite of their weaknesses, these men served God. They did the best they could with the talents (and lack of talents) they had, and in the end that is all God really asks of all of us.

Not all persons are to be great heroes of faith like Abraham and Sarah — many of us will be like Isaac and Jacob, struggling along as best we can. As long as we respond to God's call as best we can, we will still be one with Him, and God will be not only the God of Abraham, Isaac, and Jacob but also our God.

Shalom,
Fr. Jude Winkler, OFM Conv.